The Best of
Chilterns Wildlife

Pete Hawkes & Matt Kirby

The Best of Chilterns Wildlife

Pete Hawkes & Matt Kirby

First published in 2019
by Hawkes Design & Publishing Ltd

ISBN: 978-1-9998335-7-2

Contents

Introduction   2

The Chilterns   3

• Woodlands   4

• Rivers, ponds & lakes   27

• Fields & hedgerows   46

• Chalk grassland   54

• Parks & gardens   70

Photographic advice   87

Resources   89

Index   90

We have defined wildlife as all flora & fauna, including mammals, birds, amphibians, reptiles, invertebrates, fish, plants, lichens, fungi, slugs and snails.

Front cover image of Brown Hare: BEN HARTLEY. Back cover images of Ruby-tailed Wasp: EMILY HOBSON; Red Kite: CAROL SCOTT; Water Vole: MERVYN CHILTON; Common Frog: PETE HAWKES; Muntjac: ANITA CLARK; Fly Agaric: DAVID INFANTE; Sparrowhawk: GRAHAM PARSONS; Pyramidal Orchid: CHRISTOPHER PONTIN; Harebell and Common Blue Butterfly: MERVYN CHILTON

Introduction

Welcome to *The Best of Chilterns Wildlife*, a book inspired by Matt Kirby's 'Chesham Wildlife' facebook page, where local people have posted their nature photographs taken in the Chilterns. Over the years this has provided an overview of the most regularly sighted species, along with those that are particularly admired, including some prized rarities. As such it is not intended to be an encyclopedia or comprehensive guide.

The digital age has enabled practically everyone to participate and to share their images, with many reaching semi-professional standards, using a range of cameras, lenses, smartphones and photo-editing software.

Several conservation bodies, including BBOWT, the Chiltern Society, the Woodland Trust and the National Trust, manage nature reserves and Sites of Special Scientific Interest (SSSIs) and we guide readers to these in relation to different species of wildlife.

Some of the species pictured are non-native and, despite being attractive, can be a nuisance, for example the Grey Squirrel, Glis glis, Muntjac Deer and Harlequin Ladybird. Many seem to be here to stay and perhaps it is time to celebrate them; others

not depicted are so damaging that they require eradication programmes, such as Himalayan Balsam, Japanese Knotweed, American Mink and Red-eared Terrapin.

One particular aim of the book is to increase awareness and understanding of our wildlife, to help differentiate between various species, deepen our respect for nature and the countryside, and highlight human impact on the environment. We sincerely hope that you find this a useful resource whilst enjoying the Chilterns countryside.

Pitstone Windmill with the chalk grassland near Ivingoe in the background. Photographer: PAULA WESTERN

The Chilterns

The Chiltern Hills are a land of chalk, clay, flints, sands, puddingstones, sarsens and gravels which lies north-west of London, stretching from the south-west and the Thames Valley of Oxfordshire, north-east through Buckinghamshire and Bedfordshire to Hitchin in Hertfordshire. Just over half of the extended Chilterns area mapped below was designated an Area of Outstanding Natural Beauty (AONB) in 1965.

Here there lies a diversity of habitats from chalk grassland, to the UK's largest stands of beechwoods, to internationally rare chalk streams. Many of these habitats are protected within nature reserves, many others require our vigilance and careful management in order to protect the wildlife and natural beauty of this corner of England.

The darker green delineates the Chilterns Area of Outstanding Natural Beauty (AONB) as managed by the Chilterns Conservation Board. The lighter green is the extended Chilterns area specified by The Chiltern Society.

Woodlands

A Blackcap on Hawthorn at Rickmansworth. Photographer: DALE AYRES

Ancient **Beech** woodland is a major feature of the Chilterns, within which also grow **Ash, Wild Cherry, Wych Elm, Rowan, Holly, Silver Birch, Hazel** and **Yew**. The almost inexhaustible supply of timber once provided a ready source of material for the High Wycombe furniture industry. The woodlands were managed mostly by large estates and land owners who sold trees to local woodturners, known as 'bodgers,' who worked directly in the woods. Evidence of old saw pits amongst the trees is a legacy of the work carried out to convert tree trunks into planks.

Many local woodlands are managed by the Forestry Commission, National Trust or Woodland Trust. Bottom Wood, near Studley Green, has been managed by the Chiltern Society since 1984. It is a 35-acre ancient woodland dating back to before 1600 and home to over 700 different species of plants and animals. Penn Wood and Common Wood near High Wycombe are managed by the Woodland Trust but are closely watched over by the Friends of Penn Wood. Their campaign in the 1990s prevented an attempt to create a golf course on part of this 435-acre site – one of the largest ancient woodlands in the Chilterns. Oaks, Silver Birches and Rowan trees abound.

Photographer: BEN BROTHERTON

Wild Service Trees, once widespread, became rarer as old woods were cleared and are now confined to ancient places such as the Forest of Bernwood, a Royal hunting ground at Brill, Aylesbury. A favourite tree of the authors is the **Quaking Aspen**, which grows on well-drained soil near rivers and has loudly trembling leaves in all weathers. The dwarf evergreen **Box** is nationally rare. There are only three native Box woodlands in the UK and the largest of these lies on the Chilterns escarpment near Great Kimble. These steep slopes support substantial areas of unimproved chalk grassland where some **Juniper** can also be found.

Large mammals

The **Red Deer** *(Cervus elaphus)* is Britain's largest wild animal, standing four feet high at the shoulder. It is a native species, once used by Mesolithic man as a source of skins, tools and food. Thousands of years of farming cleared the great forests and Red Deer have become confined to Scotland, south-west England and a few other small, scattered populations far from the Chilterns. In past times they may well have been accompanied locally by predatory animals such as the **Wolf, Bear, Lynx, Wild Cat** and **Wild Boar.** In the 21st century the Chilterns are occupied by smaller species of deer, along with some less threatening predatory mammals.

Muntjac Deer

(Muntiacus reevesi)

Reeves' Muntjacs were first introduced to the UK at Woburn Park by the Duke of Bedford in around 1900 and later to Whipsnade Zoo. These are the ancestors of those now found in most English counties. **Chinese Water Deer** also escaped from Whipsnade but, because they thrive in reedbeds, have not migrated as far. Muntjacs are fairly small and solitary. They eat woodland vegetation and have a distinctive barking call.

Photographer: MERVYN CHILTON

Photographer: KATHLEEN LIBRA

Roe Deer *(Capreolus capreolus)*

This is the only truly indigenous deer in the Chilterns. Records of them date back to at least 6000BC. They are very shy – slipping quietly through woodlands and copses, often undetected – although they are increasingly seen entering scrubland areas closer to towns, or even large gardens where they like to eat rose plants. They tend to be solitary in summer, when their coats are a rusty red, whereas in the winter they turn a dull, slate grey colour and form small groups.

Photographer: PAUL JENNINGS

Fallow Deer *(Dama dama)*

These deer were most likely introduced by the Normans. They prefer large, open woodlands and parks, such as the Ashridge Estate near Berkhamsted. Only the male carries antlers, and indeed the stag is the symbol of Hertfordshire County Council. At Ashridge, the deer are culled on an annual basis to keep numbers in check and to reduce their negative impact on woodlands, where they eat saplings and create a 'browse line' on mature trees.

Photographer: MERVYN CHILTON

European Badger *(Meles meles)*

Badgers, our biggest land predator, are nocturnal relatives of the **Stoat** and **Weasel**, and although equally secretive, are more in evidence due to burrowing and road kill. They leave their underground sett at sunset and are very cautious, despite having no enemies except man. They are protected by law and the local Wildlife Trusts work to immunise them from TB. Badger earthworks often border farmers' land and there is an ongoing debate on their link with bovine TB.

Photographer: MERVYN CHILTON

Red Fox *(Vulpes vulpes)*

Foxes live in woods and copses, but often visit towns to scavenge from bins. They are the only wild relative of the dog in the UK. They have a bushy tail or 'brush' tipped with white. They live in holes known as dens or earths, leaving a distinctive musty smell, and hunt at night. Foxes are omnivorous, eating fruit, small mammals such as rabbits, ground birds, amphibians, large insects and eggs. The female, known as a vixen, emits a loud screaming call in the mating season.

Photographer: IAIN NIBBSY

Small mammals

Pipistrelle Bat

(Pipistrellus pipistrellus)

Bats are the only mammal that can fly. Being nocturnal they hunt, not using vision, but by making high pitched calls and using echo detection. The Pipistrelle is the smallest and most common bat of the Chilterns. Experts use electronic equipment to identify their distinctive call. There has been a decline in bat numbers, some species by 50%. They need hibernation sites and we can help by providing suitably placed bat boxes.

Photograph: WIKIPEDIA COMMONS

Grey Squirrel *(Sciurus carolinensis)*

Ubiquitous to any country walk, the Eastern Grey Squirrel was introduced to the UK in the 1870s and is now considered an invasive species; at the time they were thought of as fashionable additions to estates. After their introduction, populations spread quickly, resulting in the displacement of the native Red Squirrel. They eat tree bark, berries, seeds, nuts and fungi. Their taste for bark, particularly of young beech and oak, creates a significant problem in the Chilterns.

Photographer: SARAH MURTAGH

Hedgehog *(Erinaceus europaeus)*

This once common mammal is endangered by bonfires, and in particular by road traffic. Hedgehogs are now a priority species under the UK Biodiversity Action Plan. They are covered with a coat of sharp spines and can roll into a ball as protection from predators. They are nocturnal and also hibernate during the winter, sleeping in a specially built nest in thick undergrowth. Since 1985 the world's first bespoke hedgehog unit has been operating at Tiggywinkles Wildlife Hospital at Haddenham near Aylesbury.

Photograph: Creative Commons: PIXABAY

Edible Dormouse *(Glis glis)*

Introduced to the UK in 1902 by Lord Rothschild at Tring, its range now spreads across a triangle between Luton, Aylesbury and Beaconsfield. The name comes from the Romans, who ate them as a delicacy. It is nocturnal and herbivorous, being partial to the seeds of beech trees. It hibernates over winter and often makes its home in insulated loft spaces. They are legally protected and must be removed by specialists. The native **Hazel Dormouse** is found in the Chiltern Society's Bottom Wood, but is in decline.

Photographer: Shutterstock – MIROSLAV HLAVKO

Woodland birds

Pheasant *(Phasianus colchicus)*

This colourful game bird was probably introduced by the Romans, although it comes originally from Asia. Pheasants eat seeds, grain and insects. The males are extremely territorial, with frequent fights, and a successful cock may have a harem of hens but plays no part in the incubating or rearing of the chicks. Largely forgotten up until the 19th century, they became a popular gamebird and today there are around 37 million birds released annually by gamekeepers.

Photographer: ELENA MUTTIK

Blackcap *(Sylvia atricapilla)*

Once only a summer visitor to the Chilterns this bird has more recently remained over the winter months. The Blackcap is a typical warbler with grey upper parts and pale grey underparts. The male has a glossy black cap while the female has a copper brown cap. They are best spotted in woods or parks and gardens with plenty of tree cover. They are now on the rise in the Chilterns and two good sites are the Local Nature Reserves at Prestwood and at Gomm's Wood, High Wycombe.

Photographer: ESMOND BROWN

Tree birds

Green Woodpecker
(Picus viridis)

The UK's largest woodpecker is quite unmistakable and is often seen around beechwoods and also in churchyards, where it searches out ants' nests between the graves, using its strong beak and barbed tongue to extract the insects. They have an undulating flight and a loud, laughing call or 'yaffle'. A related bird, the **Wryneck**, also feeds on the ground on a diet of ants – a very rare bird in the Chiltern Hills.

Photographer: ANGELA SCOTT

Great Spotted Woodpecker *(Dendrocopos major)*

This medium-sized woodpecker is common in Chiltern woods. The male has red markings on the neck and head, not found on the female. It has a very distinctive bouncing flight and spends a great deal of time pecking at tree trunks to find beetle grubs and larvae. Trees that have died make idea nesting sites and the beak is used to hammer and chisel out deep nesting holes. The **Lesser Spotted Woodpecker** is much rarer locally.

Photographer: BEN BROTHERTON

Nuthatch *(Sitta europaea)*

The Wood Nuthatch is a plump, distinctively grey-blue bird, often seen running up and down the trunk of a tree or branches using its powerful feet, as it searches for insects. It has a long, powerful pointed bill, short tail and small legs. Nuthatches seldom venture far and establish their territory with loud and simple song. They particularly like to nest in old holes in mature trees – often abandoned woodpecker nests. Marlow Common is an idyllic Chiltern nature reserve where you can spot these characterful birds.

Photographer: DALE AYRES

Treecreeper *(Certhia familiaris)*

With its long, slender, downcurved bill, the Common Treecreeper is a small and very active bird, climbing woodland trees in a manner reminiscent of a mouse, but supported by a stiff, long tail. They search for insects and spiders, often starting at the bottom of a tree trunk and working their way upwards. They are solitary birds that tend to stay strictly within the boundaries of their territory. Treecreepers can be seen at Brush Hill Local Nature Reserve, east of Princes Risborough.

Photographer: DALE AYRES

Crow family

Rook *(Corvus frugilegus)*

Despite being a common bird, Rooks are rarely seen within towns. Their black feathers show a blueish-purple sheen in bright sunlight and they have bare grey skin around the bill. They gather in large social groups, with nests made of sturdy twigs at the top of large trees. Rookeries can seem dark, eerie places, especially with the clamour of the birds' raucous calls. A much larger and more solitary bird is the **Raven** *(Corvus corax)* which is getting more common locally, with regular sightings near Ivinghoe Beacon.

Photographer: PAULA WESTERN

Jay *(Garrulus glandarius)*

The colourful Jay, with its striking blue wing patches, is a shy woodland bird found throughout the Chilterns, sometimes feeding on beech-mast, the brown nuts that fall from beech trees. It's also well known for helping spread oak trees by burying its prized food, acorns. Jays can be seen in both deciduous and coniferous woodland, although they rarely move far from cover, but their raucous call will often give them away. Gomms Wood near High Wycombe is a favourite haunt.

Photographer: DALE AYRES

Jackdaw *(Corvus mondedula)*

A smaller member of the crow family, Jackdaws have black plumage with a distinctive silver grey sheen to the back of the head. A very inquisitive and intelligent bird, often showing great interest in shiny objects, they tend to live in complex social structures, nesting in chimneys and old buildings. Its call is a familiar, playful 'tchack', from which it gets its name. The **Carrion Crow** *(Corvus corone)* is an equally intelligent and social bird with all-black plumage, that gravitates towards open farmland.

Photographer: DALE AYRES

Common Magpie *(Pica pica)*

'Pied' with black and white feathers, this is considered to be one of the most intelligent birds in the UK. Often spotted amongst trees and scavenging on road-kill, they are also great garden pest destroyers, but their noisy, predatory and arrogant character has made them unpopular with many people. However, when viewed closely the black plumage takes on a more colourful appearance, with a purplish-blue iridescent sheen to the wing feathers and a green gloss to the long tail, making them worthy of further appreciation.

Photographer: INEZ COLLIER

Very small birds

Wren *(Troglodytes troglodytes)*

This iconic bird is small but stocky and extremely restless, with its short, cocked tail flicking repeatedly. For a small bird the Wren has a remarkably clear, loud voice usually ending in a trill. The male builds several nests and the female selects one that she prefers. Numbers often decline in severe cold winters but recover well due to their ability to fledge large numbers of young. They eat spiders, insects and beetles and despite being nervous and secretive, are easily seen in woodland and gardens.

Photographer: DALE AYRES

Goldcrest *(Regulus regulus)*

The Goldcrest is the smallest European bird, along with the Firecrest and comes from the kinglet family of birds. It is common in the UK in coniferous habitats and evergreen woodland, where it eats small insects, spiders, moth eggs and aphids. Its golden crest feathers have led to it being known as the 'king of the birds' in European folklore. The Chiltern Rambling Trail is part of the National Trust's Ashridge Estate, which supports a considerable diversity of wildlife including Goldcrests.

Photographer: ANDY TOWNSHEND

Firecrest *(Regulus ignicapillus)*

This tiny, restless bird has one of its UK breeding grounds at Wendover Woods in the Chilterns, where the 'Firecrest Trail' is a 2.8 mile signposted walk. Unlike the Goldcrest, it prefers broadleaf woodland trees such as oak, alder, beech and holly, but it often remains above the branches, so is harder to spot. It is also brighter and cleaner looking than the Goldcrest, with bronze-coloured shoulders. The male's orange crest is displayed vividly in the spring breeding season.

Photographers: DALE AYRES / MATT GIBSON

Long-tailed Tit

(Aegithalos caudatus)

Found across the Chilterns, this bird is easily recognisable with its very long tail and small fluffy body and tiny triangular beak. It feeds on insects and seeds and has an unusual nest: a domed structure made from moss and lined with feathers. It has complex social habits, staying in noisy excitable groups of up to 20 birds which are often seen passing through woods, hedgerows and gardens. Numbers are severely affected in winters, explaining why a clutch can be as many as 15 eggs.

Photographer: DALE AYRES

Owls

Tawny Owl *(Strix aluco)*

The Tawny Owl is the most common owl, although its numbers are reported to be in decline – it has been moved from a green to amber listing of conservation concern. It can be found in most woodlands throughout the area, in addition to large urban parks and suburban gardens. This stocky round owl is mottled reddish-brown in appearance, with a paler underside and rounded head and dark eyes. It is a nocturnal bird that hunts mainly rodents, small birds, frogs, fish, insects and worms. Tawny Owls nest in tree holes.

Photographer: LEE EVANS

Barn Owl *(Tyto alba)*

If you're lucky enough to see this owl, you'll notice its white heart-shaped face, buff back and wings and pure white underparts. It is generally nocturnal, with a silent, ghostly flight, but it is not unusual to see Barn Owls hunting for mice, voles, shrews and larger mammals at dusk and dawn. They tend to nest in cavities, abandoned barns and dense trees and can often be spotted over open grassland and agricultural fields. The oldest Barn Owl in Britain (15 years of age) was recorded in the Chilterns in 2015.

Photographer: MERVYN CHILTON

Short-eared Owl

(Asio flammeus)

Sometimes known as 'Shortie', this owl can be spotted in the daytime, especially in winter over grassland, feeding on Field Voles and small birds. Short-eared Owls have been spotted nearby, in the Harefield area and at Gallows Bridge Farm nature reserve. They usually nest on the ground in scraped-out hollows lined wth grass and feathers, and have a reputation for defending their nest and young with great ferocity. **Long-eared Owls** breed occasionally in Buckinghamshire.

Photographer: MERVYN CHILTON

Little Owl *(Athene noctua)*

This bird lives up to its name, being only 20cm in height – the smallest owl in the UK. It was introduced in the 19th century around Kent and Northamptonshire. They can be seen during daylight hours in small copses, parks and around farms, woodlands and orchards, feeding mainly on small mammals and birds. The Little Owl is a cavity-nesting species, using mainly oak, ash or fruit trees, stone walls, even nest boxes and rabbit burrows. Numbers may be declining but these owls have been breeding in Cassiobury Park, Watford.

Photographer: ANGELA SCOTT

Woodland flowers

Common Bluebell

(Hyacinthoides non-scripta)

The Common Bluebell is exclusive to northern Europe, with Britain containing more than half of the world's population. Ancient Chiltern oak and beech woodlands are often on lime-rich soil, ideal for carpets of these purplish-blue, highly scented flowers in late spring. This is a legally protected species in the UK, with the main threats being the picking of flowers and the illegal digging up of bulbs. Other threats are global warming and hybridisation with the Spanish Bluebell. Amongst the bluebells in woodland clearings look out for **Primroses, Wood Anemones, Hedge Woundwort, Dogs Mercury** and the **Early Purple Orchid** (one of the earliest flowering orchids). According to the Chilterns Conservation Board, some of the best Bluebell woods in the area are:

- Wendover Woods, near Wendover
- Adams Wood, near Lane End
- Bradenham Woods, near High Wycombe
- Ashridge Estate, near Berkhamsted
- Cowleaze Woods, near Watlington
- Ipsden Heath, near Henley-on-Thames.

Photographer: DUNCAN LUND

Ramsons *(Allium ursinum)*

Also known as Wild Garlic, this plant can be found in damp woodland areas, such as at the Yoesden Nature Reserve in the Radnage Valley. It has elliptical shaped leaves which when crushed have a strong garlic smell. An Italian chef at The Lee makes a flavoured olive oil infused with Ramson leaves. They also make a fantastic addition to salads, pesto, omelettes and potatoes, but remember to forage responsibly and that the bulbs should not be disturbed. The aroma of Wild Garlic can often fill wooded areas.

Photographer: PETE HAWKES

Coralroot Bittercress

(Cardamine bulbifera)

This is a rare plant in the UK, but the Chilterns area is one of its strongholds, where it grows on dry woodland slopes over chalk between High Wycombe (Bottom Wood) and Watford. It propagates by bulbils which drop off and take root in the decaying leaf litter. Along with **Yellow Archangel, Wood Sorrel** and **Sweet Woodruff** to name but a few, it is an ancient woodland indicator plant.

Photographer: PETE HAWKES

Orchids – woodland

Fly Orchid *(Ophrys insectifera)*

This amazing orchid *(left)* attracts wasps as pollinators, not only with its shape, but also by releasing pheromones.

White Helleborine

(Cepalanthera damasonium)

Mostly found in shady beech and hazel woods. Rarely are the egg-shaped flowers found fully opened.

Photographer: CHRISTOPHER PONTIN

Bird's-nest Orchid

(Neottia nidus-avis)

These endangered orchids are usually found in shady beech woods on limestone soil, so there are many ideal habitats in the Chilterns. They get their name from the root formation, resembling an unruly bird's nest. Some of the finest specimens are on the very steep slope in Pulpit Wood (National Trust), growing alongside various helleborines. Not to be confused with the similar looking, parasitic non-orchid, **Toothwort**.

Photographer: CHRISTOPHER PONTIN

Fly Agaric *(Amanita muscaria)*

This toadstool with its vibrant warning colour is well known from childhood fairytales. It can grow up to 20cm across. They are found in woodland where Silver Birch trees grow, and Penn Wood often hosts a good display. There is no scientific difference between a toadstool and a mushroom, but the former name is usually given to those fungi that are poisonous or inedible. Don't touch, as Fly Agaric is poisonous, and infamous for its dangerous psychoactive and hallucinogenic properties.

Photographer: GILL MORRIS

Common Puffball

(Lycoperdon perlatum)

The beechwoods are magical in autumn, when fungi form beneath fallen leaves or in tufts on dead wood. **We recommend going on a fungi foray organised by an expert who can help identify what you find**. The Common Puffball, for example, is an edible fungus, but only young specimens should be collected, as once the spore mass begins turning yellow the fungi are unsuitable for eating and it can also be confused with immature poisonous Amanita species.

Photographer: SIAN JOSETTE

Magpie Inkcap

(Coprinopsis picaceus)

Occurs most often in deciduous woodland in autumn, particularly under beech trees and oaks, the specimen featured being spotted at Ashridge. It develops from a tall egg shape to a bell shape, revealing a glossy dark background beneath the white patches. Inkcaps 'deliquesce', where the gills and cap darken and melt. The resulting black liquid can be used as an ink or a dye, though unlike the **Shaggy Inkcap**, these fungi are poisonous and best left to be admired.

Photographer: ELENA MUTTIK

White Saddle *(Helvella crispa)*

This striking mushroom, also known as the 'Elfin Saddle' can be recognised by its creamy white colour (later turning a morbid shade of leaden grey), curled cap with fuzzy underside and hollow fluted and folded stem. It is commonly found near woodland paths – this specimen was found at Pancake Wood near Ashley Green. Believed to be mycorrhizal, it provides soil with water and nutrients in return for simple sugars, acting like a secondary root system for plant roots. Not recommended for eating.

Photographer: ELENA MUTTIK

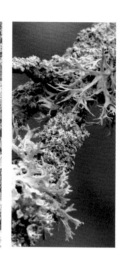

Cup Fungi *(Peziza)*

True to their name, these peculiarly shaped fungi often resemble brittle, rubbery cups. Over 50 species are known in the UK, often found growing on the ground in grassy or wooded areas. One easily spotted type is the **Orange Peel Fungus** *(Aleuria aurantia)*, the bright orange cup warped in a way that resembles an orange peel; another is the **Scarlet Elf Cup** *(Sarcoscypha coccinea)*, a vivid red cup found on decaying wood. Cup Fungi play a beneficial role in enriching soil with carbon, nitrogen and hydrogen.

Photographer: ELENA MUTTIK

Lichen

According to the The British Lichen Society, of the 2,000 British species of lichen, more than 600 have been found growing on churchyard stone. Whilst the **Golden Crustose Lichen** favours limestone memorials, the **Dotted Ramalina** is a fruticose (bushy) lichen that is widespread on trees due to its tolerance to acid and nitrogen. Lichen are useful indicators of good air quality and low pollution levels. However, the loss of ancient trees and woodlands can have negative consequences for lichen communities.

Photograph: Creative Commons – PIXABAY

Woodland butterflies

Ringlet *(Aphantopus hyperantus)*

This is a common butterfly, similar in appearance to the male **Meadow Brown**. It gets its name from the rings on its hindwings. It is one of the few butterflies that flies on overcast days; this is because its colouration helps it to warm up quickly. The spots can vary in number and size. They will feed at bramble and wild privet flowers for their nectar. They can be found in damp grassland and on woodland edges, along with another of the 'brown' butterflies: the two-tone **Gatekeeper**.

Photographer: PETE HAWKES

Speckled Wood
(Pararge aegeria)

This common butterfly is divided into multiple sub-species. They are often found in woodland as well as in gardens and hedges, particularly in sunny clearings where the male will sit in wait to attack intruders. Generally they prefer damp habitats. The markings vary depending on location within the country. The southern UK population are dark brown with orange spots. Both males and females visit tree tops to collect honeydew and as such are disinclined to feed on flowers.

Photographer: PETE HAWKES

Rivers, ponds & lakes

View over Stockers Lake,
Rickmansworth.
Photographer: RAY FOX

Chalk streams are an internationally rare habitat with more than 85% of such rivers flowing through England. The main chalk streams of the Chilterns are the Ver, Gade, Bulbourne, Chess, Misbourne, Hughenden Stream, Wye and Hamble Brook.

They are fed from natural underground aquifers that store rainwater which has soaked through the chalk. They spring with high water clarity, generate gravel river beds and create a habitat that fosters an abundance of insects, fish, plants and small mammals, many of which are under threat.

Chiltern chalk streams often flow through towns, where the water course has been modified for agriculture or industry, creating restrictions to wildlife. Further damage is caused by abstraction of water for homes and industry. Chalk streams have winterbourne sections at their headwaters which are often dry for part of the year as a result of low rainfall or over-abstraction.

Most of the chalk streams have volunteer groups to help conserve and manage them. **The Chilterns Chalk Streams Project** works to improve the river habitat as a whole.

The area supports a number of other aquatic habitats, including lakes, gravel pits, reservoirs, canals and ponds. These too are vitally important for a range of species, including amphibians and wetland birds.

Flora

Loddon Lily *(Leucojum aestivum)*

These stunning plants, also dubbed 'Summer Snowflakes', are a speciality of damp woodland in Berkshire and Oxfordshire, often seen along the River Loddon and the Thames Path. A good place to see them is the Withymead Nature Reserve near Goring-on-Thames, in the far south-west region of the Chilterns. They also thrive in damp meadows, rather like another Oxfordshire speciality, the **Snakeshead Fritillary** with its nodding, chequered blooms. Well worth a trip out to see them both.

Photograph: Creative Commons – PIXABAY

Watercress *(Nasturtium officinale)*

Watercress is an aquatic or semi-aquatic perennial plant native to Europe and was first cultivated for profit at the beginning of the 19th century. However, it is one of the oldest-known leaf vegetables eaten by people. The Watercress industry flourished along the River Chess in Victorian times, using chalk-filtered water from artesian wells. It was dispatched in hampers by train to London. For health reasons it is best to eat freshly grown commercial watercress. There are Watercress beds at Ewelme, managed by the Chiltern Society.

Photograph: Creative Commons – PIXABAY

Water Crowfoot

(Ranunculus penicillatus)

A plant synonymous with Chiltern chalk streams, where it provides shelter for fish and invertebrates from predators. It is an aquatic buttercup with several sub-species that are difficult to tell apart. The presence of the long, trailing tresses of Water Crowfoot in fast-flowing streams is vital in helping maintain a clear gravel bed. Excessive river management can disrupt this balance. The River Chess at Chenies is an ideal location to see this plant.

Photograph: WIKIPEDIA COMMONS

Orchids – marsh

Southern Marsh Orchid

(Dactylorhiza praetermissa)

There are localised colonies of these orchids growing in the Chess Valley, close to the River Chess and in the ancient Frogmore Meadows, near Chenies. They thrive in wet soil, meaning that much of their range has been reduced with land drainage. The **Early Marsh Orchid** *(right)* may be found at Weston Turville Reservoir. These rare orchids are a very pale pink to flesh colour, and enjoy the same wet meadow habitat.

Photographer: CHRISTOPHER PONTIN

Marsh Helleborine

(Epipactis palustris)

An excellent colony of these pretty orchids is hidden away in the Chilterns at Pitstone Fen Nature Reserve. A key to this Reserve may be obtained from the office at College Lake reserve. They are plants of wetland areas, which produce their loose flower spikes in sunlit areas during July and August. This orchid is in decline due to land drainage, and is considered extinct in Bedfordshire. However, in the right conditions, it can thrive.

Photographer: CHRISTOPHER PONTIN

Carnivorous insects

Southern Hawker

(Aeshna cyanea)

There are about 30 **Dragonfly** species in the UK, including hawkers, chasers, darters and skimmers. The large Southern Hawker is commonly seen; it breeds in small ponds but often hunts well away from water. It appears to be very inquisitive and will often fly towards the observer, making it a good subject for close-up photography. The male has additional blue colouring. To help stem the loss of Dragonfly habitat, consider creating a wildlife-friendly garden pond.

Photographer: KATHLEEN LIBRA

Banded Demoiselle

(Calopteryx splendens)

Of the 20 species of **Damselfly** in the UK this is perhaps the most beautiful – also known as the 'Kingfisher' or 'Water Butterfly'. The male, pictured, is blue and green, or all blue, and the female is metallic green and bronze. It can be seen in flight during the summer months, mainly along slow-flowing streams, particularly those with muddy beds, for example on the River Chess at Sarratt, Hertfordshire. It is seen here eating a Mayfly.

Photographer: PETE HAWKES

Amphibians

Common Frog

(Rana temporaria)

Distinguishable from toads by their smooth, moist skin and long legs used for jumping or hopping, frogs are almost always found in damp habitats. They are regular visitors to garden ponds, hibernating in winter in mud or under log piles. The metamorphosis from frogspawn to tadpole to frog is miraculous, especially for children, and pond dipping is regularly organised by the local Wildlife Trusts. Frogs have limited protection by law.

Photographer: PETE HAWKES

Common Toad *(Bufo bufo)*

Toads generally have shorter legs than frogs; they prefer to crawl rather than hop and spend less time in water. Their warty skin and golden eyes also distinguish them. If threatened, a toad can puff itself up to appear bigger. At Oaken Grove Wood, thousands of toads migrate to a lake on the other side of the Henley to Marlow road. Volunteers collect them and take them across the road to safety to reduce those killed by passing traffic. This is one of the largest assisted migrations in the country.

Photographer: PETE HAWKES

Great Crested Newt

(Triturus cristatus)

This is Britain's most strictly protected amphibian, due to the loss of its habitat, which is specifically ponds around farmland and old earthworks, where they can over-winter on land. It is the nation's largest newt, with both sexes having an orange belly and fine white spots on their flanks; the male has a jagged crest. Survey sites are ponds at Penn Wood, near High Wycombe and at Little Wittenham, north of Wallingford.

Photographer: Shutterstock – TIBERIU SAHLEAN

Smooth Newt

(Lissotriton vulgaris)

This is a more commonly occuring newt which hibernates in damp areas, emerging in March to breed in ponds. Surveys have been taken at Dundale Wildlife Site north of Tring and at Naphill Common, where the **Palmate Newt** was also found. The male Smooth Newt has a wavy crest, whereas the male Palmate has only a protruding filament the length of its tail. Female Smooth and Palmate Newts are similar in their light brown colouring.

Photograph: WIKIPEDIA COMMONS

Fish-eating birds

Grey Heron *(Ardea cineria)*

This tall wading bird is easily recognisable, both when seen completely still – hunting for fish, ducklings and small mammals – and in flight with its almost two-metre wing span and outstretched legs. Although often solitary, they nest in colonies known as heronries and become more social when roosting in tall trees, reed beds and bushes. Heronries can be found at Stockers Lake, Rickmansworth, on Drayton Bank at Wilstone Reservoir and at Rushmere Park, Leighton Buzzard.

Photographer: JUREK JUREKN

Little Egret *(Egretta garzetta)*

This bird is a recent colonist, now seen regularly on and around Chiltern waterways. Measuring 55 to 65cm in height, its plumage is almost entirely white with plumes on its crest, back and chest during the breeding season, black legs and yellow feet. This egret stalks its prey, mainly of fish and frogs, in shallow water, often running with raised wings and shuffling feet. The Meades Water Gardens and the length of the River Chess in Chesham are good places for easy sightings.

Photographer: PAULINE WINTER

Great White Egret *(Ardea alba)*

Standing almost one metre tall and with black feet (unlike the yellow feet of the Little Egret), this wading bird has a slow flight with neck retracted and legs extended. It feeds on fish, frogs and insects with the death blow delivered with a quick thrust of the sharp bill. Numbers have steadily increased in the UK in the last twenty years, with sightings in the Chilterns extended area at Boxmoor near Hemel Hempstead, the River Chess and at Maple Lodge Reserve, Rickmansworth.

Photographer: PAULA WESTERN

Kingfisher *(Alcedo atthis)*

The most brilliantly coloured of British birds with its iridescent turquoise and metallic copper plumage. It has a distinctive shrill call as it flies low over water, hunting for fish. It nests by burrowing into river banks. The Boxmoor Trust reserve and Wilstone Reservoir near Tring are superb bird watching spots. These large, man-made lakes with reedbeds, boggy ground, willow and alder trees make ideal territory, and Kingfishers are a good indicator of a healthy freshwater ecosystem.

Photographer: ANDREW BROWN

Waterfowl

Domestic Duck

(Anas platyrhynchos domesticus)

Domesticated ducks can often be seen living freely on ponds in parks and gardens. They were originally bred from the **Mallard**, primarily for egg and meat production. Two white varieties are the **Pekin Duck** and the larger **Aylesbury Duck**. The latter has its last farmed breeding site in Chesham, but was once commonly seen on Buckinghamshire's rivers. It is the source of Beatrix Potter's character 'Jemima Puddle Duck' .

Photographer: DALE AYRES

Mallard *(Anas platyrhynchos)*

The most familiar duck in the Chilterns, the Mallard is a common sight near water. The drake has a glossy green head, maroon-brown chest and grey on the body, with a yellow bill. Female Mallards are brown and speckled, with an orange bill. Both have iridescent blue feathers called a speculum on their wings. Mallards tend to congregate in groups, searching for water plants, seeds, acorns, berries and insects. They nest in a variety of sites from grassy riverbanks to flat roofs.

Photographer: PAULINE WINTER

Mute Swan *(Cygnus olor)*

The Swan is the largest of our waterfowl. It flies with neck extended and regular, slow, dramatic wingbeats. Serious issues with lead poisoning have now been solved by banning lead in anglers' weights. They eat water plants, snails and insects. The swan forms the central symbol of Buckinghamshire County Council, and 'Swan Upping' takes place in July on the River Thames at Marlow – a 12th century tradition dealing with the conservation and Royal ownership of swans.

Photographer: KATHLEEN LIBRA

Greylag Goose *(Anser anser)*

The ancestor of the domestic goose, it is now outnumbered by the **Atlantic Canada Goose**, which in some locations has become a nuisance, and even by the **Egyptian Goose** at Medmenham. It has mottled and barred grey & white plumage, an orange beak and pink legs and can be seen in parks, gravel pits and rivers throughout the Chilterns, and especially in low-lying grassy fields in river valleys. Most are semi-tame, having been reintroduced in the 1930s and 1960s.

Photographer: RAY FOX

Crakes and rails

Coot *(Fulica atra)*

A familiar bird of our lakes, ponds and rivers, with a distinctive bright white beak and featherless 'shield' above, giving rise to the expression 'bald as a coot'. They swim confidently in open water and despite having strong legs that allow them to walk and run vigorously (they are often spotted running noisily over the water before taking off) these birds spend most of their time on the water diving for food, which includes small invertebrates. Look out for their large untidy-looking nests in the spring.

Photographer: CHRISTOPHER PONTIN

Moorhen *(Gallinula chloropus)*

Although closely related to the Coot, this bird spends most of its time out of the water and can even climb trees; it is far more secretive and nervous. Moorhens are omnivores, eating everything from snails and insects to wild berries. They appear to be placid, but will nevertheless defend their nests with ferocity. They are also seen as a sedentary bird, often staying local to where they were hatched, but under the cover of darkness they do sometimes take to the air searching for new habitats.

Photographer: GRAHAM PARSONS

Water Rail *(Rallus aquaticus)*

This shy, secretive bird is smaller than the Moorhen and more often heard than seen. It is found in reedbeds and freshwater wetlands all year round, hiding amongst the vegetation. It has mainly brown upperparts with blue grey face and underparts, black & white barred flanks and long reddish bill, used to probe in mud and shallow water. Water Rails are omnivorous, feeding on insects, seeds, larvae, small fish and snails during the summer, and plant matter during the winter.

Photographer: DALE AYRES

Green Sandpiper

(Tringa ochropus)

A secretive wading bird and a passage migrant, spotted in the Chilterns feeding around the edges of flooded gravel pits, lakes and rivers, but never breeding here. Nervous and vigilant, they frequently bob up and down when standing and fly in a zig-zag pattern when disturbed. They rarely use their bill for probing mud, but prefer to pick invertebrates from the surface of the water. Their blackish-green upperparts are generally much darker than other sandpiper species.

Photographer: DALE AYRES

Wetland birds

Grey Wagtail *(Motacilla cinerea)*

A very colourful bird often spotted in the Chilterns on fast flowing rivers near lowland farms, including on the River Chess in Chesham. Like all the wagtails it has a very long, constantly wagging tail. It has a distinct flying pattern with a low, undulating and bobbing style. It tends to eat ants and midges found beside rivers, as well as snails and tadpoles in the shallow water, and it nests in hollows and crevices lined with moss and twigs. Not to be confused with the **Yellow Wagtail**, which is less common locally.

Photographer: BEN BROTHERTON

Reed Bunting
(Emberiza schoeniclus)

Similar in size and appearance to a House Sparrow, the male has a black head, white collar and drooping white moustache; females have a streaked head and are lighter brown. Often found in wetlands with dense vegetation, they spend the winter months on farmland looking for seeds. It has been in rapid decline since the 1970s, but good locations to see them include Weston Turville Reservoir nature reserve, Marsworth Reservoir and the nearby River Loddon in Berkshire.

Photographer: BRIAN RIDGLEY

Great Crested Grebe

(Podiceps cristatus)

The largest member of the grebe family and a most elegant, graceful bird. Extensive hunting for its feathers almost led to its extinction, but the population has dramatically recovered. They have dagger-like bills ideal for catching a wide range of fish when diving, often with underwater chases. They are well known for an elaborate courtship involving both birds rising out of the water and shaking their heads. Very young Grebes can be seen riding on their parents' backs in the water.

Photographer: BRIAN RIDGLEY

Mandarin Duck *(Aix galericulata)*

One of the most distinctive water birds with its striking orange colouring, it was introduced from the Far East and has become established in the wild. This is one of the few non-native species that has not created environmental problems, mainly because it inhabits areas, such as small wooded ponds, not favoured by indigenous wildfowl. They nest in trees high above the ground. Good locations are Black Park near Slough, Tring Reservoirs, the Wendover Canal, the lakes at Burnham Beeches and the Halton Canal.

Photographer: BRIAN RIDGLEY

Sinensis Cormorant

(Phalacrocorax carb sinensis)

A large bird with a hook-tipped bill that dives underwater to find its food. They are larger than the similar **Shag,** with a less delicate bill and more yellow around the face. They are also a social bird, nesting in groups, mainly in trees. The best locations for Cormorant colonies are Stockers Lake, Rickmansworth and Wilstone Reservoir, Tring. Unlike seabirds, the Cormorant does not have natural oil in its feathers, so it spends a lot of time fanning and drying its wings.

Photographer: SARAH HOW

Common Tern *(Sterna hirundo)*

Within the Chilterns the Common Tern can be seen between April and September at Stockers Lake, a former gravel pit in the Colne Valley near Rickmansworth, where they breed on the islets and also at Marsworth Reservoir near Tring. Unfortunately their eggs and young are vulnerable to predation by mammals such as rats and by larger birds including gulls, owls and herons. They have a graceful flight and hover over the water, plunging down for fish, earning them the nickname 'Sea Swallow'.

Photographer: MERVYN CHILTON

Black-headed Gull

(Chroicocephalus ridibundus)

Gulls have been gradually moving further inland for breeding and roosting. This is the commonest inland gull, found on ploughed land and also in wetland areas. Large, noisy flocks eat worms, insects, fish, carrion and kitchen scraps. The influx of **Lesser Black Backed Gulls** has proved to be more damaging to local wildlife.

Winter plumage

Photographer: LEE EVANS

Fish

The River Wye from High Wycombe to Bourne End and on to the River Thames has a good stock of the indigenous **Brown Trout**.

The River Misbourne from Great Missenden and through Amersham to the River Colne has suffered in recent years from reduced or no flow. When the flow returns the first colonists were reportedly **Sticklebacks** and, later, **Bullheads**.

The River Chess which springs from three sources in Chesham is increasingly dry through the town, but navigable downstream alongside the popular Chess Valley Walk and on to the Colne.

Rainbow Trout inhabit the Chess, having originally escaped from fisheries during much of the 20th century. This is one of just a few self-sustaining populations in the country. Also present are **Chub Fry, Graylings** and **Minnows**.

Many invasive and non-native species have made their way into our waterways in recent times, including American Signal Crayfish, Red-eared Terrapin and Zebra Mussels. These intruders compete with indigenous species for food and can spread infectious diseases to our own wildlife.

Brown Trout *(Salmo trutta)*

This fierce, predatory fish lives in fast-flowing rivers with gravel beds such as the Wye and Chess. Brown Trout have also been found in the River Gade in Hemel Hempstead following work by the Environment Agency to restore the river's natural chalk stream characteristics.
It feeds with sharp pointed teeth on insect larvae, small fish and flying insects. The young fish, called 'fry', hatch and feed on their yolk sac. Brown Trout can live for 20 years, but many die after spawning.

Photograph: WIKIPEDIA COMMONS

Rainbow Trout

(Oncorhynchus mykiss)

A fish native to North America which was introduced to UK waters for commercial farming. However, within the Chilterns it has become naturalised in the River Chess where it feeds on insects, larvae, damselflies and mayflies. This beautiful, torpedo-shaped member of the salmon family is a silvery colour with bright blue, pink and green highlights on its flanks. It lives for an average four to six years and can tolerate poorer quality water than the Brown Trout.

Photographer: PAUL SHAW

Mammals

Water Vole *(Arvicola amphibius)*

Immortalised as 'Ratty' in *The Wind in the Willows*, this is Britain's fastest declining mammal. The culprit is the American Mink which escaped from fur farms. Chiltern conservationists have helped buck the national trend, with Water Vole populations remaining on the River Chess, the River Misbourne and at Ewelme. Since 2001, Mink control has resulted in substantial population recovery, but close monitoring, as well as habitat enhancement on the River Misbourne, is ongoing to maintain this success story.

Photographer: MERVYN CHILTON

Otter *(Lutra lutra)*

The once common Otter was absent from the Chilterns by the 1970s due to pollution and habitat loss. Recent sightings in the Grand Union Canal near Linslade and in the Rivers Wye and Misbourne are encouraging, with cleaner water now that many pesticides have been banned. Otters travel vast distances and need a network of waterways. Environmental groups have helped by building artificial breeding places, or holts. Non-native Mink are smaller, with a round, fluffy tail compared to the broad-based, flat tail of an Otter.

Photograph: Creative Commons – PIXABAY

Fields & hedgerows

Ox-eye Daisies at Pednor, Chesham.
Photographer:
PETE HAWKES

Mammals

Brown Hare *(Lepus europaeus)*

In many cultures, the Hare is a symbol of fertility. In spring when the usually shy and nocturnal Hare comes into open fields for breeding, the females can be seen 'boxing' with the males. This is to test the males' perseverance or to show they are not yet ready to mate. The breeding season runs from January to August and a female can produce 12 offspring a year. Their natural predators include domestic cats, foxes, domestic dogs and birds of prey. They can run at over 40mph to escape predation.

Photographer: MERVYN CHILTON

Rabbit *(Oryctologus cuniculus)*

Introduced to Britain in the Middle Ages, the Rabbit will spend much of its life in a network of burrows, also called warrens. Grazing animals, including Rabbits, perform a number of important roles in maintaining the chalk grassland ecosystem of the Chilterns. One of the most vital jobs is to consume the young shoots of saplings and trees, preventing them from growing, which allows other plant species access to sunlight and soil nutrients. This stops the area turning into scrub and woodland.

Photographer: BRIAN RIDGLEY

Summer visitors

House Martin *(Delichon urbicum)*

Arriving from Africa in April and leaving in September, this highly social bird can be identified by its blue-black upper parts, pure white underparts and forked tail. It spends much of its time on the wing, collecting flying insects. It constructs a mud nest below the eaves of buildings. Uniquely, the young from the first brood are often observed helping the parents feed the next brood, with three generations sleeping in the same nest. Look out for colonies in early autumn gathering on rooftops ready for the long migration.

Photographer: DALE AYRES

Swallow *(Hirundo rustica)*

Related to House Martins and Sand Martins, these birds are part of the 'hirundine' family. The Swift is similar looking but unrelated. Swallows are small birds with dark, glossy-blue backs, red throats, pale underparts and long, deeply forked tails, with an agile flight as they catch insects, often over water. Having spent most of their time in South Africa they arrive here in the spring to nest, choosing barns, garages, cow sheds and the eaves of rural buildings. They are a welcome sight in the skies over the Chilterns.

Photographer: DALE AYRES

Sand Martin *(Riparia riparia)*

These birds arrive from North Africa in March and leave in August. They can be spotted at Springfield Quarry, Beaconsfield and Grovesbury Pit, Leighton Buzzard. They have sandy-brown upperparts with white underparts and a brown breast band, with slightly forked tail. They nest in colonies, sometimes as many as 1,000 pairs, digging burrows in steep sandy banks around water. Their population has been stable here despite droughts in Africa affecting the supply of winter insects, their main source of food.

Photographer: DALE AYRES

Common Swift *(Apus apus)*

A remarkable bird that sleeps, eats and mates on the wing. It has a plain dark brown, compact body with long, curved, scythe-like wings. Swifts can easily be identified by their screaming call as they fly acrobatically above towns and waterways throughout the summer, having arrived from Africa in early May and prior to departing in August. They can travel at speeds of 70mph and will cover 500 miles in a day eating mainly insects. They nest in the eaves of buildings such as churches and old properties.

Photograph: CREATIVE COMMONS

Field birds

Skylark *(Alauda arvensis)*

This bird features in works of literature and music due its unrivalled songflight. The male rises vertically with rapid wingbeats, then hovers and sings on high for up to one hour before 'parachuting' back down to earth. Over the last 30 years there has been a 76% decline in Skylark numbers due to changes in farming practice. The RSPB advises farmers on ways to encourage birds such as Skylarks. The beautiful **Yellowhammer** is also under threat due to fewer seed food sources available on farmland.

Photographer: DALE AYRES

Lapwing *(Vanellus vanellus)*

Nicknamed the 'Peewit' due to its distinctive call, this bird can also be recognised in flight by its broad, blunt, rounded wing shape. It is predominantly black & white but its wings have an iridescent green and purple sheen, and there is a characterful crest on the back of its head. This ground nesting bird needs low disturbance areas to breed, for example meadows adjoining wetlands, which is a common habitat in the Vale of Aylesbury. Populations have declined nationwide and numbers are low in the Chilterns.

Photographer: CHRISTOPHER PONTIN

House Sparrow

(Passer domesticus)

This noisy, sociable bird is often seen nesting, feeding and bathing in large groups. Once a common bird, general numbers have been in significant decline. The reason for this is a mystery and theories range from loss of suitable nesting sites to pollution and even mobile phone radiation. Attempts were made in the Victorian era to eliminate this bird via 'Sparrow Clubs' which were involved with thousands of culls, but thankfully this robust bird continues to survive.

Photographer: BRIAN RIDGLEY

Dunnock *(Prunella modularis)*

Despite sometimes being called a Hedge Sparrow, this bird is in fact not related to the House Sparrow. They can be seen moving quietly along the ground, feeding on insects, worms, berries and seed. They have an attractive blue-grey head and breast and constantly flick their tails as a territorial warning. Dunnocks have extraordinary mating patterns. The female will mate with several males within her breeding territory to ensure there is an adequate supply of food, and more than one male will feed the chicks.

Photographer: PAULINE WINTER

Grasses & flowers

Meadow Foxtail

(Alopecurus pratensis)

Chiltern grassland consists mainly of close-grazed, species-rich turf, whereas wetland areas support grasses, sedges and rushes. Hay meadows can be exceptionally rich in wildflowers, with the grassy sward including meadow species such as **Sweet Vernal-grass** and **Red Fescue**. Meadow Foxtail is a tufted grass of fertile, moist meadows – an important habitat for invertebrates – one example being Frogmore Meadows SSSI north of Chenies.

Photographer: PETE HAWKES

Greater Stitchwort

(Stellaria holostea)

Look for these delicate star-shaped flowers in woodlands, along hedgerows and on roadside verges from April to June. It is one of the commonest spring flowers and plays a major part in the charm of Chiltern woodlands at bluebell time. The stems are quite brittle, the leaves are grass-like and the plant does not do well in waterlogged sites. It once had the derogatory common name 'Poor Man's Buttonhole'.

Photographer: PETE HAWKES

Common Poppy *(Papaver rhoeas)*

This plant is closely linked with farming, as it thrives in ploughed soil. It probably first appeared in the Chilterns with Stone Age farmers. Also known as Corn Poppy, Corn Rose, Field Poppy, Flanders Poppy or Red Poppy, this flower is mostly associated with commemorating soldiers who sacrificed their lives in the World Wars. Their symbolic meaning of new life dates back to the time of the Romans who created poppy garlands to worship their gods and ask for fertility of their crops. Poppies contain rhoeadine which is toxic to livestock if eaten in large quantities. They can be found on roadsides, arable land and waste places. Poppies can reappear after years of being treated with herbicide sprays as the seeds are very resilient, surviving in the ground for at least 80 years before germinating.

Photographer: PETE HAWKES

Chalk grassland

Ivinghoe Beacon.
Photographer:
JUREK JUREKN

The Chilterns AONB has over 700 hectares of chalk grassland. It is of national importance, being a unique and fragile habitat supporting plants that fail to thrive elsewhere, for example certain species of orchid, as well as the Chiltern Gentian and Pasque Flower. Many unusual species of insect are attracted to these plants, including the **Adonis Blue** *(pictured)* and Duke of Burgundy butterflies.

The plant-rich short turf, or 'sward', of chalk grassland is not entirely natural, having evolved over the centuries as a result of grazing by domestic livestock, especially sheep, and also rabbits. This well-balanced ecosystem includes predators, which in turn keep rabbits from over-grazing.

Since 1945 the UK has lost more than 80% of its chalk grassland to changes in farming practice and urban development. Chalk scrub, despite being of wildlife value and sometimes consisting of rarities such as Box and Juniper, needs active management to control its spread. Conservation and volunteer groups across the Chilterns work to maintain, restore and expand these landscapes, which are popular with both local residents and visitors alike for leisure and relaxation, as well as being being vital for much of our wildlife.

A selection of the best chalk grassland in the Chilterns:

- Pegsdon Hills, near Barton-le-Clay
- Aldbury Nowers, near Tring
- Ivinghoe Beacon, near Ivinghoe & Aldbury
- Dunstable Downs and Whipsnade Estate
- Coombe Hill, near Wendover
- Pulpit Hill, near Princes Risborough
- Grangelands, near Princes Risborough
- Aston Rowant, near Watlington
- Hartslock, near Goring-on-Thames

Photographer: GRAHAM SMITH

Butterflies

Chalk Hill Blue

(Polyommatus coridon)

Found exclusively on chalk downland where there is a profusion of wild flowers, such as at Hartslock Nature Reserve, Goring and at Aston Clinton Ragpits. Apart from the rare **Large Blue**, the Chalk Hill Blue is the UK's largest blue butterfly. Sometimes groups of males will be attracted to animal dung, where they can get moisture and minerals. The larvae feed on Horseshoe Vetch and the adults prefer Knapweed and Scabious. See also the **Common Blue** on the back cover.

Photographer: MERVYN CHILTON

Marbled White

(Melanargia galathea)

With such distinctive markings this is unlikely to be mistaken for another species. It occurs in large numbers on flowery grassland and can often be spotted in July. If you look closely you may find them on tall grass stems, where the adults like to roost. They have a preference for purple flowers such as thistles. Red Fescue is particularly important for the caterpillars, as they feed on this species of grass. Look out also for **Meadow Brown** and **Gatekeeper** butterflies in this group of 'Browns'.

Photographer: MERVYN CHILTON

Silver-washed Fritillary

(Argynnis paphia)

This butterfly is large and a particularly strong flyer. The males have 'sex brands', which are distinctive black veins on their forewings which they use in courtship, where the male sprinkles the female with scented scales. The adults feed on the nectar produced by brambles and thistles. The caterpillars eat Common Dog Violet. In southern parts of England, a small percentage of the females have a stunning bronze-green tinge to their wings, which is known as the Valezina form.

Photographer: ANDY TOWNSHEND

Duke of Burgundy

(Hamearis lucina)

A small butterfly which lives in groups on grassland, such as at Ivingoe. In England they are found mostly in central-southern areas, making them a Chilterns speciality. The males are most often seen; the females keeping low. The eggs are laid on the underside of Primrose and Cowslip leaves. Numbers have declined in recent years. The **Purple Emperor**, an even more elusive but very large butterfly, has been spotted at the NT Bradenham estate, Tring Park and Wendover Woods.

Photographer: GRAHAM SMITH

Birds of prey

Red Kite at West Wycombe. Photographer: ANNE WEBBER

Red Kite *(Milvus milvus)*

The Chiltern Hills are one of the best locations to see these elegant birds, with their wingspan of almost two metres. Having been driven to near extinction, there are now an estimated 1,000 breeding pairs across the area after a reintroduction project that began in 1989 at Ibstone near Stokenchurch and Shirburn near Watlington – one of the most successful conservation projects of the 20th century. It eats mostly carrion and small mammals. Where food is plentiful, a large number can be found living together.

Photographer: BEN BROTHERTON

Buzzard *(Buteo buteo)*

This majestic bird has had a chequered past in the UK with the population significantly affected by man. In the last few decades, alongside the introducton of Red Kites, numbers have increased significantly. Listen out for its distinctive 'mew' call in contrast to the Red Kite's rapidly repeated 'weoo-weoo-weoo'. This bird has broader rounded wings and a shorter tail in comparison, which fans out when soaring on thermals of warm air. They pair for life and are opportunistic predators that take a variety of prey.

Photographer: DALE AYRES

Kestrel *(Falco tinnunculus)*

Kestrels may be seen in a range of habitats from open countryside to the outskirts of towns, but are most easily spotted hovering, with pointed wings, over the verges of the M40 and M1, searching with exceptionally good eyesight for their prey of small mammals in the long grass. Another favourite spot is the steep escarpment slope of the Dunstable Downs. Kestrels are in decline, so National Trust countryside rangers are erecting nest boxes and monitoring the young birds.

Photographer: BEN BROTHERTON

Sparrowhawk *(Accipiter nisus)*

These birds of prey have adapted their usual woodland hunting grounds in the Chilterns to farmland with trees and copses, and even to gardens. The alarm calls of smaller birds dashing for cover may indicate their presence, although they are amazingly silent and agile in flight, sometimes taking a bird as large as a Wood Pigeon by surprise. The male has a bluish-grey back and wings whereas females, which are slightly larger, have brown wing plumage.

Photographer: GRAEME KENNEDY

Peregrine Falcon

(Falco peregrinus)

A large, powerful bird with long, pointed wings and a relatively short tail, the Peregrine Falcon was at a low point in the 1960s due to both human persecution and pesticides in the food chain. Although still illegally persecuted, numbers have recovered and can now be seen at Tring Reservoirs and in urban areas, including Aylesbury, where nesting platforms have been erected. Peregrines are the fastest creature on the planet – this agile hunting bird can reach speeds of over 200mph as it dives. It often catches its prey, especially pigeons, in mid-flight.

Photographer: IAIN NIBBSY

There have also been sightings of **Osprey** at Weston Turville and Chenies, and this photograph of a **Hobby** was taken at Startop's End Reservoir, Tring.

Photographer: DALE AYRES

Reptiles

Slow Worm *(Anguis fragilis)*

Despite looking like a worm or a snake, this is in fact a legless lizard. It is well camouflaged, but when fortunate enough to observe one, you'll notice that it blinks with its eyelids. A natural territory is heathland where slugs and worms can be found to eat, but they are often seen in mature gardens and allotments, where compost heaps make a safe home. However, if there are domestic cats around, these reptiles are unlikely to be present. Warburg and Gomm's Wood nature reserves are good habitats for these reptiles.

Photographer: JEAN DANECKER

Common Lizard

(Zootoca vivipara)

Isolated Lizard colonies are still to be found in patches of unimproved Chiltern chalk grassland or areas maintained for wildlife, such as the Chairborough Road Nature Reserve at High Wycombe. They can be spotted basking on logs when not hunting for insects and worms, which they shake before swallowing whole. A Lizard has the ability, when threatened by a bird of prey, to shed its tail, which will continue twitching and distract the predator.

Photographer: BRIAN RIDGLEY

Grass Snake *(Natrix natrix)*

The longest snake in the UK, but totally harmless to humans. A fully-grown adult may be more than a metre in length. They favour damp grassland and gardens, especially those with ponds, where they hunt amphibians, fish, small mammals and birds. Volunteers with the Chiltern Rangers collect mounds of freshly cut grass to provide over-wintering and breeding opportunities for these snakes. All UK reptiles are protected from killing and injuring by humans under the Wildlife and Countryside Act.

Photographer: MERVYN CHILTON

Adder *(Vipera berus)*

Where Adders once thrived on the open heaths and commons of the Chilterns, the fragmentation of habitats through agriculture and urbanisation has led to a very serious decline in numbers. However, they are now a legally protected species and BBOWT's Warburg Reserve is a refuge for these venomous snakes. They bask in spring sunshine, tightly coiled after shedding their skin, displaying their zigzag patterning. Although Adders have no hearing, they can sense vibration, lying in wait to ambush prey.

Photographer: EMILY HOBSON

Snails & slugs

Spiders

Roman Snail *(Helix pomatia)*

Crab Spider *(Misumena vatia)*

There are 30 species of slug and 100 species of snail in the UK. This is the largest of the snails, with a body up to 10cm long and a shell up to 45mm in width. (The **Ashy-Grey Slug** can be up to 25cm in length). They were introduced to the UK by the Romans, but their distribution is mostly limited to the Chilterns, North Downs and Cotswolds. They live for up to 20 years on undisturbed chalky grassland, for example at Aston Clinton Ragpits, where they are fully protected by law.

Photographer: CHRISTOPHER PONTIN

Spiders are not insects (which have six legs and three main body parts) but are classified as arachnids, which have eight legs. Crab Spiders do not create webs, like the familiar **Garden Spider**, but instead they wait on flowers for insects to land, then pounce on them with their crab-like front legs. A mature female has the chameleon-like ability to gradually change the colour of her body through white, yellow and green to match her surroundings. The males are smaller with brown legs. Found mainly in southern England.

Photographer: PETE HAWKES

Grassland flora

Pasque Flower

(Pulsatilla vulgaris)

This pretty spring flower is associated with Good Friday and Easter celebrations. It is a rare flower in the Chilterns and indeed nationally scarce, requiring undisturbed calcareous grassland to grow, but it can be seen at Knocking Hoe Nature Reserve in Bedfordshire and at Ivinghoe Beacon. Cultivated specimens can easily be found in garden centres, so tread carefully if you are lucky enough to see this flower and do not disturb.

Photographer: CHRISTOPHER PONTIN

Chiltern Gentian

(Gentianella germanica)

The county flower of Buckinghamshire. It seeds on to bare earth, so grazing land is required, making it a national scarcity and a local speciality, mainly confined to the Chiltern chalk downs. This habitat has been threatened since WWII, but thankfully the local Wildlife Trusts restore unimproved grassland areas, for example at Chinnor Hill. Its biennial, trumpet-shaped flowers appear from August to September.

Photograph: WIKIPEDIA COMMONS

Orchids

The Chiltern Hills are a stronghold for orchids, and certainly one of the best places to see them. They thrive on the poor soil of the downland, rich in chalk, as well as in damp meadows (see page 30) and woodlands (see page 22). The area has 35 of the 56 species recorded in the British Isles.

These are wonderfully exotic and unusual plants. Many are symbiotic with soil fungus, others attract pollinators with amazing mimicry. Orchids grow in specific habitats, so their survival is linked with farming and land management, hence many are thriving in protected areas at local nature reserves.

Several orchids are known as 'Helleborines' (see flowers below). A **Red Helleborine** at a reserve near Princes Risborough was the only one to flower in the UK in 2017. Other Helleborines such as the **White, Violet, Narrow Lipped** and **Green Flowered** grow sparsely in Chiltern woodlands.

Common Spotted-orchid

(Dactylorhiza fuchsii)

A relatively widespread orchid that grows in a range of soils, but which favours chalk grassland and roadside verges. The name comes from the exotic-looking spotted leaves. It flowers from late spring in varying shades of lilac, and sometimes produces a pure white form. The **Heath Spotted-orchid** is similar, but grows in more acidic soils.

Photographer: CHRISTOPHER PONTIN

Bee Orchid *(Ophrys apifera)*

This easily recognisable orchid has been adopted as Bedfordshire's county flower and may be found throughout the Chilterns on chalk grassland, as well as in meadows, and in damp conditions close to rivers and lakes. The flowers have evolved to attract male bees as pollinators, which try to mate with it and then unwittingly carry the pollen to the female part of the next Bee Orchid they visit. Good populations are found at Dunstable Downs and at Homefield Wood, Marlow.

Photographer: CHRISTOPHER PONTIN

Pyramidal Orchid

(Anacamptis pyramidalis)

To the left is the Pyramidal Orchid, a late flowering variety that is common on Chiltern chalk grassland. The pyramid-shaped flowers become more oval in time, but each plant takes five to ten years to mature. To the right is the **Chalk Fragrant-orchid** *(Gymnadenia conopsea).* Head to Aston Clinton Ragpits in June to see this delicate orchid in abundance. The sweet-smelling fragrance increases in the evening to attract moths.

Photographer: CHRISTOPHER PONTIN

Musk Orchid *(Herminium monorchis)*

The small but attractive Musk Orchid grows amongst the grass close to the Ridgeway Path at Grangelands and Pulpit Hill Nature Reserves. In fact, at least ten species of orchid may be found on this land managed by the National Trust – a great place to start your orchid hunting. These rare Musk Orchids are unassuming and easily overlooked, as is the **Frog Orchid** and the more common, heavier set and equally musky orchid, the **Common Twayblade.**

Photographer: CHRISTOPHER PONTIN

Military Orchid *(Orchis militaris)*

Homefield Wood, near Marlow, has a wonderful colony of these sweet smelling orchids *(left)*. Orchid hunters and botanists travel far and wide to see these flowers, the petals of which resemble a knight's helmet.

Man Orchid *(Orchis anthropophora)*

Another rare and nationally scarce orchid, with flowers resembling a tiny figure, it can be found at Totternhoe Knolls in Bedfordshire.

Photographer: CHRISTOPHER PONTIN

Lady Orchid *(Orchis purpurea)*

Hartslock Nature Reserve, near Goring-on-Thames, is a very important site for orchids, both locally and nationally. In the foreground, to the left, is the Lady Orchid, red listed as endangered, usually a solitary specimen. On this steep slope, the equally vulnerable **Monkey Orchid** *(Orchis simia),* shown as a hybrid to the right, also grows. The flowers form a shape like the long arms and legs of a monkey. These two types of orchid have been known to hybridize.

Photographer: CHRISTOPHER PONTIN

Burnt Orchid *(Neotinea ustulata)*

Knocking Hoe National Nature Reserve in Bedfordshire, right on the northern edge of the Chilterns, is looked after by Natural England and is a Site of Special Scientific Interest (SSSI). This is home to the only local colony of this endangered plant, also known as the 'Burnt-tip Orchid'. They are counted every year, even the non-flowering plants, and fenced off to protect them from hungry rabbits. It can be 10 to 15 years before the stem develops from seed.

Photographer: CHRISTOPHER PONTIN

Parks & gardens

Juvenile fly on
Aquilegia plant.
Photographer:
PETE HAWKES

There are an estimated 27,000 public parks and green spaces in the UK, along with over 16 million gardens and allotments. Together they form a huge sanctuary for wildlife, but the way we manage them can have a significant impact.

Installing bird boxes in high, sheltered sites away from cats; leaving piles of stones and logs to encourage hedgehogs and toads; or putting up a 'bug hotel' for over-wintering insects are all good initiatives.

Many gardeners are going organic. Compost can be made from kitchen and garden waste; rotted down in a compost bin, a sweet-smelling, friable material is produced that is equal to any garden centre alternative. Furthermore, in buying peat-based composts from retailers, the destruction of peat bogs and their associated wildlife is set to continue. A compost heap may also provide a habitat for Slow Worms.

You can help Honey Bees and other insects to thrive by allowing space for wildflowers and plants rich in nectar. Sometimes bees swarm and form large clumps (often the size of a football) on tree branches. If you see a swarm of bees, contact a beekeeper or swarm collector who will provide helpful advice. To find out more contact the British Beekeepers' Association.

Bees are very important pollinators of fruit and vegetables.

The best way of bringing new life into the garden is to dig a pond. Rather than buying goldfish, allow frogs, toads and newts to find their own way to the water, or introduce tadpoles. During the night amphibians will often move around the garden eating slugs and snails, a great aid to the gardener.

Photographer: PETE HAWKES

Butterflies

The Butterfly Conservation charity divides butterflies up into several clear groups. The Orange-Tip, right, is one of the most attractive butterflies of the WHITES & YELLOWS. The Small Tortoiseshell and Peacock are grouped within the EMPERORS, VANESSIDS and FRITILLARIES along with other commonly seen garden butterflies: the **Comma, Red Admiral** and **Painted Lady**. The Silver-washed Fritillary on page 57 is one of a large number of similar looking Fritillary species. Among the BROWNS are the Ringlet and Speckled Wood on page 26, and also – slightly confusingly – the Marbled White on page 56. The HAIRSTREAKS, COPPERS and BLUES are a beautiful group of small blue or bright brown butterflies, of which we have included the Adonis Blue on page 55 and the Chalkhill Blue on page 56. The Duke of Burgundy (page 57)

stands alone as a METALMARK, and finally the SKIPPERS are represented here by the **Small Skipper** (*Thymelicus sylvestris*)

Photographer:
BRIAN RIDGLEY

Orange-tip

(Anthocharis cardamines)

The Orange-tip is a beautiful and delicate butterfly. Despite the name, only the males have orange tips to their wings. They can be spotted on warm spring days, from April to June. Males will live their entire lives at the forest edge, whereas the more reclusive females prefer meadows. Cuckoo Flower and Hedge Garlic provide ideal laying sites for the female's orange eggs. Orange-tip caterpillars are cannibalistic, and may eat another of their own species should they meet!

Photographer: PETE HAWKES

Small Tortoiseshell

(Aglais urticae)

A well-known and commonly found species, often spotted in gardens. It is one of the first butterflies to be seen in spring in large numbers around flower beds. Males will compete for nest space during flight to assert dominance. One male will try to fly above another, which will then try to dive and climb to escape. After a certain distance is reached, they will split and one will return to the nest and the other will carry on, looking for another location.

Photographer: JUSTINE FULFORD

Peacock *(Aglais io)*

The pattern of colours and eyespots of the Peacock evolved to confuse or startle predators and it is one of the most commonly known butterflies and very easy to recognise. The underside of the wings is dark and resembles wood bark, giving it excellent camouflage when hibernating. It can also produce a hissing sound by rubbing its wings together to ward off predators. They gravitate towards Buddleia plants in the garden. In terms of diet, the adults drinks nectar from flowers and the caterpillars eat nettles.

Photographer: PETE HAWKES

Birds with distinctive colouring

Pied Wagtail *(Motacilla alba)*

This delightful small, long-tailed and rather sprightly black & white bird, when not standing and frantically wagging its tail up and down, can be seen dashing about over lawns or car parks in search of insects. It frequently calls during its undulating flight and often gathers at dusk to form large roosts in town centres. They build their nests in holes in walls, buildings and abandoned larger nests, using grass and moss. The male and female both incubate the eggs and feed the young.

Photographer: PAULA WESTERN

Robin *(Erithacus rubecula)*

This well-known plump bird with its bright orange-red breast, face, throat and cheeks is often associated with the winter months, although they can be seen year round. The males are noted for their highly aggressive behaviour and are relatively unafraid of people, being drawn to human activities involving the digging of soil – feeding on insects, snails and worms. Their mournful song is very distinctive and beautiful. The robins at Amaravati Buddhist Monastery at Great Gaddesden are particularly tame.

Photographer: GRAHAM PARSONS

Blue Tit *(Cyanistes caeruleus)*

Easily recognisable with its striking blue and yellow plumage, smaller in size than the **Great Tit**, this is one of the most attractive of our garden visitors. They feed mostly on insects, especially caterpillars and beetles, but can often be seen on bird tables feeding on seeds, peanuts and suet food. This, along with the provision of nest boxes, has helped the population to increase. They also nest in holes in trees and walls, even letter boxes, and are well known for their agility.

Photographer: BRIAN DUMPLETON

Goldfinch *(Carduelis carduelis)*

A strikingly colourful small finch which uses its slender beak to extract seeds from plants, helped by its short legs, enabling it to hold tight and swing acrobatically. From the brink of extinction, mainly due to it being kept as a cage bird, populations have now recovered. In the winter they can be seen in flocks searching for seeds and insects, although some migrate as far as southern France and Spain to avoid the harsh winters. An equally striking finch is the male **Linnet**, with its red-pink breast in summer.

Photographer: DALE AYRES

Thrushes & starlings

Song Thrush *(Turdus philomelos)*

A familiar bird of parks, gardens and scrub land, slightly smaller than the Blackbird, but with a similarly beautiful, loud, repetitive song that is frequently mentioned in poetry and literature. They are well known for smashing snail shells by striking them against a stone with a flick of the head. Their dark speckles look like arrows pointing towards the head with fewer, smaller dark spots than the **Mistle Thrush**. Numbers of both thrushes have declined, probably due to agricultural intensification and the removal of hedgerows.

Photographer: DALE AYRES

Redwing *(Turdus iliacus)*

Mostly seen between September and April – arriving from a hazardous crossing, often at night, from Iceland, Russia and Scandinavia. They roam the countryside feeding on worms, fruit and seasonal berries. They are identified by a broad, creamy white stripe over the eye and an orange-red underwing. Redwings are social birds, often gathering in huge flocks, which can include the similar looking **Fieldfare**, another migrant. They maintain contact with each other with their high-pitched flight calls.

Photographer: BRIAN RIDGLEY

Blackbird *(Turdus merula)*

A very common sight in suburban areas, well known for its harmonious song, even during rainfall. In the winter, resident birds are joined by migrants from Scandinavia, the Baltics, Russia and Germany. They are fond of feeding on lawns with their heads cocked to one side, listening for Earthworms. An ability to switch to different foods as the seasons change is part of their success. The female is brown in colour. The **Ring Ouzel** is a rare visitor from upland areas that resembles a Blackbird but has a white crescent across the breast.

Photographer: DALE AYRES

Starling *(Sturnus vulgaris)*

Although still a common bird, numbers are unfortunately in decline. They look almost black from a distance, but when viewed closely are seen to have a beautiful purple and green metallic sheen, speckled with white. Starlings come together at dusk, sometimes forming a huge flock with amazing aerobatics known as a 'murmuration', as seen at Marsworth Reservoir, Tring. As the light fades part of the flock plunges down to roost. With such large groups they attract the attention of predators such as Sparrowhawks.

Photographer: MERVYN CHILTON

Insects

There are more than 20,000 insect species in the UK. At least one member from the following insect orders is represented by photographs in this book.

1. Flies (Diptera)
2. True Bugs (Hemiptera)
3. Grasshoppers & crickets (Orthoptera),
4. Bees, wasps & ants (Hymenoptera)
5. Butterflies & moths (Lepidoptera) (see also pp.26, 55-57, 72-73)
6. Beetles (Coleoptera)
7. Dragonflies & damselflies (Odonata) (see p.31)
8. Mayflies (Ephemeroptera) (see p.31)
9. Earwigs (Dermaptera) & cockroaches (Dictyoptera)

Advances in digital photography and macro lens technology have brought the world of insects closer to our eyes.

Earwig photograph: WIKIPEDIA COMMONS

Dotted Bee-fly

(Bombylius discolor)

Flies are rarely a favourite form of wildlife, but the tiny, patterned and fluffy Bee-fly is an uncommon and characterful insect. However, they do have a gruesome habit of laying their eggs into the nests of solitary mining bees. The larva hatches and waits for the bee larva to swell up and then feeds on its body fluids, eventually killing it. The long proboscis is used for drinking nectar – this fly is totally harmless to humans. They often bask in south-facing, sunny spots in gardens.

Photographer: EMILY HOBSON

True Bug *(Orthops campestris)*

There are almost 2,000 species of *Hemiptera* or True Bugs. All have a piercing beak, used like a hypodermic needle, to suck juices from plants or other animals, and often have long antennae and hardened, overlapping front wings. *Orthops campestris* is a tiny and quite common bug often found on umbellifer plants, with a curious, green, heart-shaped motif. They are approximately 4mm long. Adults overwinter and mate in the spring; the new generation arrives by the summer.

Photographer: PETE HAWKES

Speckled Bush-cricket

(Leptophyes punctatissima)

Grasshoppers and crickets are most familiar to us when in long grass, but can be found in a range of habitats. Bush-crickets can be distinguished by their long antennae. Pictured is the commonest Bush-cricket, with a length of 9-18 mm. The green body is covered in tiny black spots. Females have a large scimitar-shaped appendage at their rear – this is an ovipositor used to deposit eggs. They are herbivorous, feeding on a range of vegetation.

Photographer: PETE HAWKES

Bumblebee *(Bombus pascuorum)*

There are roughly 250 species of Bumblebee in the world and 24 of these exist in the UK. The majority of sightings are of the eight common species: the Buff-tailed; White-tailed; Garden; Red-Tailed; Early; Common Carder *(pictured);* and the Tree & Heath. Wild flowers and many crops rely heavily on Bumblebees for pollination, and with numbers falling across Europe due to various factors, such as habitat destruction and the use of pesticides, it is expected that the countryside could change dramatically as a result.

Photographer: PETE HAWKES

Honey Bee *(Apis mellifera)*

The European (or Western) Honey Bee is most commonly used for honey production. They originate from eastern Africa. Other products made by beekeepers include wax for making candles, lip balm, furniture polish and for waterproofing shoes; as well as propolis, which allegedly has health benefits, and is used to treat cold sores, colds and flu. A colony usually contains three types of bee: one queen (a fertile female), several thousand drones (fertile males) and tens of thousands of workers (sterile females).

Photographer: PETE HAWKES (See also page 71)

Hoverfly *(Syrphus ribesii)*

There are over 280 species of Hoverfly in the UK, belonging to the family *Syrphidae* and many are common in Chiltern gardens – sometimes also named 'Flower Flies' or 'Syrphid Flies', often brightly coloured. This colouration can mean that they are confused with wasps and bees, but they have no sting and are to be considered an asset for a gardener, as their larvae eat aphids. The adults feed on nectar, while the larvae eat a variety of foods, from decaying plants and animal matter to aphids and thrips.

Photographer: PETE HAWKES

Ruby-tailed Wasp

(Chrysis ruddii)

This wasp is solitary and can be difficult to spot as it is so small – hardly 10mm in length – but look out for it locally at Berkhamsted Castle, where it likes the sand and soft rock. It is an excellent pollinator. There are multiple species that look very similar, but they all have metallic colouration in reds, blues, bronzes and greens. They are parasitic on other wasps and bees, invading nests as part of their life cycle.

Photographer: EMILY HOBSON

Moths

Moths and butterflies are closely related, both belonging to the order *Lepidoptera*. There is very little difference between the two, apart from the butterfly's distinctive clubbed antennae. Over 2,500 species of moth have been recorded in the UK, but fewer than 70 butterflies. Moths vary greatly in appearance and size, ranging from huge **Hawk-moths** to tiny **Micro-moths**. They may not be considered as beautiful as butterflies, but they make a wonderful source of study.

Photographer: EMILY HOBSON

Emperor Moth

(Saturnia pavonia)

An intensely coloured and highly patterned day-flying moth seen in early spring. Males exhibit shades of brown with vivid orange underwings and are often mistaken for butterflies. Females are a blueish grey colour often found at rest in vegetation during the day. Females rarely fly unless disturbed and usually take flight only once mated. They lay their eggs on heathland plants, as found at Coombe Hill near Wendover.

Photographer: EMILY HOBSON

Mint Moth *(Pyrausta aurata)*

This very small and dainty moth has two broods a year: in May/June and July/August. It gets its name from its use of Mint *(Mentha)* as a food plant, though it can also be found feeding on Meadow Sage and Catnip. Ironically, Mint is usually listed as a moth deterrant. As well as in gardens, they can be found in a range of habitats: limestone and chalk grassland, woodland and marshland, as well as by water. They will fly both in the daytime and the evening.

Photographer: PETE HAWKES

Six-spot Burnet Moth

(Zygaena filipendulae)

The distinctive markings make this day-flying moth easy to find. They produce hydrogen cyanide, which makes them taste bad to predators, and in large enough doses can be fatal. They are attracted to flowery grassland and a range of flora, including Bird's-foot Trefoil, Scabious and Knapweeds. Look out also for the similarly coloured **Cinnabar Moth** with its black & yellow-striped caterpillars feeding on Ragwort.

Photographer: BRIAN RIDGLEY

Beetles

Mint Beetle

(Chrysolina menthastri)

These small native beetles grow up to 10mm long. They are a jewel-like iridescent green and are peppered with tiny indentations. The larvae and adults feed almost exclusively on various species of Mint *(Mentha)*, including Water Mint. They occur in southern England and are most likely to be found during August and September. Another similar looking species is an iridescent blue colour and called the **Blue Mint Beetle** *(Chrysolina coerulans)*.

Photographer: PETE HAWKES

Rosemary Beetle

(Chrysolina americana)

The Rosemary Beetle is a non-native species originally from southern Europe. It is thought to have been brought into the UK through plant imports, being first spotted at RHS Wisley in Surrey, and is rapidly colonising South East England and beyond. A beautifully coloured beetle, it is mainly found on Rosemary and other Mediterranean herbs such as Lavender, Sage and Thyme, and as such is unlikely to be popular with gardeners.

Photographer: EMILY HOBSON

Fat-legged Beetle

(Oedemera nobilis)

This tiny flying beetle is common in the south of England and is often found in spring, feeding on the pollen of flowers such as Sedges, Bindweed, Figwort and Poppies. The males are easier to spot than the females due to their iridescent metallic-green colouring and thicker thighs. They contain a poisonous substance called cantharidin which is used as a defence against predators. It is also known as the 'Swollen-Thighed Beetle' or 'Flower Beetle'.

Photographer: PETE HAWKES

Glow-worm *(Lampyris noctiluca)*

One of the more unusual residents of the Chilterns, the Glow-worm is in fact a type of beetle. The wingless female luminesces (emits light without heat) from its abdomen to signal to the male. The adult beetles do not feed, and live for about two to three weeks. After mating, the female stops glowing, lays its eggs and dies. Glow-worms typically favour limestone or chalky areas with long grass, and good places to find them are College Lake near Tring and Dancersend Nature Reserve at Aston Clinton.

Photographer: EMILY HOBSON

Seven-spot Ladybird

(Coccinella septempunctata)

The Seven-spot is the Ladybird we are all familiar with and can be found across the Chilterns and the rest of the UK, although they are in decline. They help manage garden pests such as aphids, so putting up a bug box is worthwhile as it will encourage them. Their bright red colouration wards off predators and they sometimes secrete a yellow liquid from their joints that can stain your hands if you try to handle them.

Photographer: EMILY HOBSON

Harlequin Ladybird

(Harmonia axyridis)

The non-native Harlequin is one of the most invasive insects, arriving in the UK from Asia in 2004. They are powerful competition to our native Seven-spot Ladybird, as they can eat more aphids and will consume other Ladybirds' larvae and eggs, making it increasingly common in our towns and gardens. It can also breed more often, giving it another advantage. Over 100 different pattern variations have been observed.

Photographer: PETE HAWKES

Photographic advice

BEN HARTLEY

Ben is currently at University studying Marine & Natural History Photography, and has a major interest in wildlife conservation. He comes from Chartridge near Chesham, Bucks, from where he walks into local woodland and the Pednor Valley AONB to capture images of land mammals – a speciality being hares. The book cover image took three months of patient waiting, without the use of a tripod. He uses a Nikon D500 camera, and the hare was photographed with a 70-300 lens in April 2017. Ben's hare photography has appeared in Countryfile Magazine. His website is at: www.benhartleyphoto.com

BEN BROTHERTON

Ben is a young professional photographer and videographer who uses a wealth of equipment and has a broad technical knowledge, having gone straight into work from A-levels.Most low light and wide angle shots are taken with a Canon 6D camera. Close-ups and action shots are taken with a Canon 7D MkII, and a favourite lens is the 500mm. He also takes images on his iPhone; in fact, he generally uses whatever equipment is at hand. Photo processing is done on a MacBook Pro, using Adobe Lightroom and Photoshop. Ben finds solace in the tranquility of wildlife photography, and spends much time hiking around the Chess Valley in Bucks and the Rye Meads RSPB Reserve in Herts. He prefers solitary nature photography expeditions and prefers not to use a tripod, allowing him to explore wild areas freely. Find out more at www.benbrotherton.com

DALE AYRES

Dale lives in Rickmansworth, Herts, not far from the Aquadrome, Stockers Lake and the Maple Lodge Nature Reserve (members only); the perfect locations for photographing water birds. Dale has always loved nature and photography, but only had the opportunity and time to combine the two activities when he retired in 2013. Ornithology is his speciality, and he carries either a Nikon D4S full frame camera or a Nikon D500 with a 600 F4 prime lens, or his 'walkabout' lens, which is a 200-500 zoom lens, with regular use of a monopod and tripod, to take some of the considerable weight. According to Dale, a quick shutter speed is essential when photographing birds, as is good lighting and composition – especially important is the 'catchlight' reflection in the bird's eye. Dale uses Adobe Lightroom to process his pictures, but prefers not to digitally manipulate the images, apart from cropping the shots where necessary. Dale is an active member of Watford Camera Club and enjoys sharing his work with others, which is often used by the RSPB and has appeared in their publications and on the BBC's 'Countryfile' programme. His work can also be seen at: flickr.com (search for Dale Ayres).

CHRISTOPHER PONTIN

Chris has lived in the Chilterns for over 60 years, and since his teenage years has been passionate about wild orchids. He uses a Pentax K100D, with various dedicated macro lenses, as well as small magnifying lenses which screw into the filter thread. He takes an interest in the Hardy Orchid Society and the Bedfordshire Orchid Group, and spends much of his time searching for orchids in the local area, as well as in Kent. Favourite locations are Homefield Wood, Marlow and the Chess Valley.

MERVYN CHILTON

For over five years Mervyn has been using a Nikon D500 camera with a 150-600 telephoto lens to capture images of deer, badgers, owls, kingfishers and numerous other elusive species. He uses a tripod to capture the perfect image, without using Photoshop enhancements. Favourite locations are Wendover Woods, the Ashridge Estate, Aldbury Nowers, Tring Reservoirs, Aston Clinton Ragpits and the chalk downland of Ivinghoe and Dunstable. See more of his work at flickr.com.

EMILY HOBSON

Emily is a primary school teacher, who enjoys promoting wildlife to the children. She grew up in Bovingdon, Hertfordshire, where the local clay pits inspired her early love of nature. Her greatest fascination is for invertebrates, and in particular moths. Of the 2,500+ moth species in the UK, she has so far recorded over 450 in the Chilterns. Emily uses a Sony A6000 camera with 30mm macro lens, or sometimes a Canon 18-200mm lens. It's important for her to use a ring flash at the end of the lens to prevent shadowing in macro work. She also uses a Panasonic TZ100 as a point and shoot camera, and even her iPhone with an Ollo-clip for close-ups. She enjoys wildlife gardening, to encourage the species that she loves.

BRIAN RIDGLEY

Brian specialises in landscape and wildlife photography. He favours full frame Canon equipment (usually the 5D) with macro, medium-telephoto and zoom lenses, always with a tripod for landscapes. Favourite locations are Tring Reservoirs, Burnham Beeches and the Hughenden Estate. He favours an early start – 4am in the summer – to capture the best light, with less pollution and more wildlife on the move. Another good time for a clear image is after a rain storm. Only minor Photoshop work is carried out. Brian is a member of the Amersham Photographic Society and a Licentiate of the Royal Photographic Society (LRPS).

Acknowledgements for research/proofing

With grateful thanks to Sophie Honeybelle, Lee Evans, Emily Hobson, David Infante, Ruth Malleson, Christopher Pontin, Elena Muttik, Stuart King, Trevor Brawn and Ken Austin.

Resources

BIBLIOGRAPHY

50 Years 50 Species
ISBN 978-1-8743574-3-8
BBOWT, edited by Helen Walsh
Pisces Publications, 2010

**A Guide to Finding Orchids in Berkshire,
Buckinghamshire and Oxfordshire**
ISBN 978-1-874357-57-5
Peter Creed, Rachel Hudson
Pisces Publications, 2013

Bugs Britannica
ISBN 978-0-7011818-0-2
Peter Marren, Richard Mabey
Chatto & Windus, 2010

**Collins Complete Guide to
British Mushrooms and Toadstools**
ISBN 978-0-0072322-4-6
Paul Sterry, Collins, 2009

Great Crested Newt Conservation Handbook
ISBN 0952110644
Tom Langton, Catherine Beckett, Jim Foster
Froglife, 2001

**The Living Land –
A Natural History of the Chilterns**
ISBN 0902875272
Michael Smith. Spurbooks Ltd, 1973

Treasures of the Chilterns
ISBN 0952110644, Tony Hyde, Ken Poyton,
Cic Upcott. The Chiltern Society, 1999

Where2Go4Wildlife in Bucks, Berks & Oxon
ISBN 978-1-8743572-7-7
BBOWT / The Nature Bureau, 2003/4

Where to See Wildlife in Britain & Ireland
ISBN 978-0-0082619-5-5
Christopher Somerville, Collins, 2017

Wild Flowers in the Chilterns
ISBN 978-0-7112278-0-4
Laurie Fallows, Gay Fallows. Frances Lincoln, 2007

Wild Orchids of Bedfordshire
ISBN 978-0-9506521-9-1
Richard Revels, Chris Boon, Graham Bellamy
Bedfordshire Natural History Society, 2015

GROUPS

www.bbowt.org.uk
www.britishbugs.org.uk
www.bucksbirdclub.co.uk
www.bumblebeeconservation.org
www.butterfly-conservation.org
www.chilternrangers.co.uk
www.chilternsaonb.org
www.chilternsblog.co.uk
www.chilternsociety.org.uk
www.fishpal.com
www.nationaltrust.org.uk
www.plantlife.org.uk
www.prestwoodnature.org.uk

Index of common names (pictured species only)

Adder 63

Adonis Blue 55

Aquilegia 70

Badger (European) 8

Banded Demoiselle 31

Barn Owl 18

Bee Orchid 67

Bird's-nest Orchid 22

Blackbird..............................77

Blackcap 11

Black-headed Gull 43

Bluebell (Common) 20

Blue Tit 75

Brown Trout 44

Bumblebee 80

Burnt Orchid 69

Buzzard................................59

Chalk Hill Blue 56

Chiltern Gentian 65

Common Blue ....back cover

Common Puffball..................23

Common Spotted-orchid 66

Coot 38

Coralroot Bittercress.............21

Cormorant (Sinensis)............42

Crab Spider...........................64

Cup Fungi 25

Damselfly 31

Dotted Bee-fly......................78

Dragonfly..............................31

Duck (Domestic)...................36

Duke of Burgundy...............57

Dunnock 51

Early Marsh Orchid...............30

Earwig 78

Edible Dormouse..................10

Emperor Moth 82

Fat-legged Beetle 85

Firecrest 17

Fly Agaric.............................23

Fly Orchid............................22

Fox (Red)................................8

Frog (Common)....................32

Glow-worm 85

Goldcrest 16

Goldfinch..............................75

Goose (Greylag) 37

Grass Snake 63

Great Crested Grebe 41

Great Crested Newt 33

Great Spotted Woodpecker..12

Great White Egret 35

Greater Stitchwort 52

Green Sandpiper 39

Green Woodpecker..............12

Grey Squirrel 9

Grey Wagtail 40

Hare (Brown)........................47

Harlequin Ladybird 86

Hawthorn 4

Hedgehog.............................10

Hedge Sparrow 51

Helleborine 66

Heron (Grey) 34

Hobby...................................61

Honey Bee 80

House Martin 48

House Sparrow 51

Hoverfly................................81

Jackdaw................................15

Jay 14

Kestrel 60

Kingfisher 35

Lady Orchid..........................69

Lapwing................................50

Lichen 25

Little Egret 34

Little Owl 19

Lizard (Common) 62

Loddon Lily 28

Long-tailed Tit....................17

Magpie (Common)...............15

Magpie Inkcap 24

Mallard 36

Man Orchid.........................68

Mandarin Duck 41

Marbled White....................56

Marsh Helleborine...............30

Meadow Foxtail 52

Military Orchid 68

Mint Beetle 84

Mint Moth 83

Monkey Orchid 69

Moorhen 38

Muntjac Deer 6

Musk Orchid 68

Newt 33

Nuthatch (Wood) 13

Orange-tip 72

Otter...................................45

Ox-eye Daisy 46

Pasque Flower.....................65

Peacock (Butterfly) 73

Peregrine Falcon...................61

Pheasant 11

Pied Wagtail........................74

Pipistrelle Bat 9

Poppy (Common).................53

Pyramidal Orchid.................67

Rabbit..................................47

Rainbow Trout 44

Ramsons 21

Red Deer 6

Red Kite 59

Redwing 76

Reed Bunting 40

Ringlet 26

Robin 74

Roe Deer 7

Roman Snail.........................64

Rook 14

Rosemary Beetle 84

Ruby-tailed Wasp 81

Sand Martin 49

Seven-spot Ladybird 86

Short-eared Owl...................19

Silver-washed Fritillary 57

Six-spot Burnet Moth 83

Skylark 50

Slow Worm..........................62

Small Skipper 72

Small Tortoiseshell...............73

Smooth Newt 33

Song Thrush 76

Southern Hawker..................31

Southern Marsh Orchid........30

Sparrowhawk.......................60

Speckled Bush-cricket 79

Speckled Wood....................26

Starling 77

Swallow...............................48

Swan (Mute) 37

Swift (Common) 49

Tawny Owl...........................18

Tern (Common)....................42

Toad (Common) 32

Treecreeper (Common).........13

True Bug 79

Watercress 29

Water Crowfoot....................29

Water Rail 39

Water Vole...........................45

White Helleborine 22

White Saddle 24

Wild Garlic...........................21

Wren 16

Notes